How To Set Goals For Yourself

How To Set Goals Successfully And Accomplish Them In 6 Simple Steps

(3-Week Action Plan Included)

Kennedy Felix

Your Free Gift

As a way of thanking you for the purchase, I'd like to offer you a complimentary gift:

- **5 Pillar Life Transformation Checklist:** This short book is about life transformation, presented in bit size pieces for easy implementation. I believe that without such a checklist, you are likely to have a hard time implementing anything in this book and any other thing you set out to do religiously and sticking to it for the long haul. It doesn't matter whether your goals relate to weight loss, relationships, personal finance, investing, personal development, improving communication in your family, your overall health, finances, improving your sex life, resolving issues in your relationship, fighting PMS successfully, investing, running a successful business, traveling etc. With a checklist like this one, you can bet that anything you do will seem a lot easier to implement until the end. Therefore, even if you don't continue reading this book, at least read the one thing that will help you in every other aspect of your life. Grab your copy now by clicking/tapping here or simply enter http://bit.ly/2fantonfreebie into your browser. Your life will never be the same again (if you implement what's in this book), I promise.

How To Set Goals For Yourself

PS: I'd like your feedback. If you are happy with this book, please leave a review on Amazon.

Introduction

With the high percentage of people who fail at setting, executing and accomplishing goals, it would be tempting to think goal achievement is some form of secretive art that only a few should realistically master.

There are many reasons why so many people fail to set or accomplish their goals. To some, the idea of setting goals seems daunting. You could say that the very idea of organization and taking their lives seriously scares them.

Others actually get down to setting goals, but when they are ready to get down to achieving them, they are unable to do so. There are also those who are a step ahead of the latter two: those who have an idea of their aim, but manage to turn their goals into enemies by aiming too high and swamping themselves with unrealistic volumes of work, or aiming too low.

Yes, goal setting is a delicate affair that requires personalization; however, setting and achieving goals in not rocket science. It is easy enough once you understand how the process works. The content in this book will equip you with the knowledge you need to set and achieve goals.

Table of Contents

Your Free Gift _____ 2

Introduction _____ 4

Introduction to Goal Setting and Its Importance _____ 7

Step 1: Pinpoint And Set Realistic Goals ___ 9

    The First Step Is Always The Hardest _____ 10

Step 2: Set Up And Execute That All-Important Yet Difficult First Step _____ 12

Why Most People Cannot Achieve Their Goals _____ 15

    Step 3: Avoid Analysis Paralysis & In So Doing, Avoid The Slacker's Doom _____ 16

Maintaining Energy And Motivation _____ 18

    Step 4: Revitalize Your Energy _____ 19

Tapping Into The Conscious Mind _____ 21

    Step 5: Enhance Conscious Awareness Of Your Goals _____ 22

Leaping Over Inevitable Blocks _____ 24

    Step 6: Overcome Creative Blocks _____ 24

Accomplishing Your Goals: 3-Week Action Plan _____ 26

   Day 1 to Day 3 _____ 26

   Day 4 to Day 6 _____ 28

   Day 7 to Day 9 _____ 29

   Day 10 to Day 12 _____ 30

   Day 13 to Day 15 _____ 33

   Day 16 to Day 18 _____ 34

   Day 19 to Day 21 _____ 35

Conclusion _____ 37

Do You Like My Book & Approach To Publishing? _____ 38

   1: First, I'd Love It If You Leave a Review of This Book on Amazon. _____ 38

   2: Grab Some Freebies On Your Way Out; Giving Is Receiving, Right? _____ 38

   3: Check Out My Other Books On Productivity _ 38

Introduction to Goal Setting and Its Importance

Goal setting is an enviable skill, a skill we all need to learn. Why is goal setting the most valuable skill you could ever have? Here are reasons why:

It brings organization into your life

If you intend to get anything done, and if you intend to establish any sort of status in life, organization is one of the key components you need. By setting goals, you know what you want from life. Even if you already know this, setting goals allows you greater intimacy with your goals and greater association with your aims. This allows you to do two things: one, drop all useless activities that previously took up your time, and two, limit expending your energy on unimportant things and instead, focus your energy on what really matters.

It allows you to focus

The problem with living a disorganized life and having no goals is that it becomes very easy to ignore very important aspects of your life. When you are disorganized, your life has no direction; thus, it becomes easy to exert too much effort and attention on things that have zero bearing on your life.

By setting goals, you exercise greater control over your life. You view everything broadly. The result is usually a higher quality life.

Goal setting improves your social, emotional, physical, and psychological life

When you set goals, you streamline your attention and your efforts. Streamlining your priorities will automatically spur personal growth in a number of ways. It will also compel you to cut off all ties with social elements and people that add no value to your life. This disconnection will help you eliminate the emotional, physical, and psychological tendencies that get in the way of a wholesome life.

Goal setting ensures you don't waste time

Once wasted, you cannot get back time. Do you know life's most open secret? It is that with every passing second, you get closer to your death. In this regard, time is of the essence. Goal setting allows you to see time as an advantage rather than a disadvantage.

Now that you know why goal setting is such an important aspect of your life, let us detail a 7-step process you can use to set and achieve goals:

Step 1: Pinpoint And Set Realistic Goals

The first step towards setting and actualizing goals is asking yourself where you want to be in the next five years: paint a broad vision. This broad vision should encompass everything, even the sentimental stuff.

Here is an example: if you intend to buy a brand new red truck, for whatever personal or business reasons, write it down. Consider everything, be it new people, a family perhaps, a good house or a better neighborhood. Include all this in your list. Take as much time as you need on this one.

* Take every activity of the day and hold it in light to your broad vision

What are you doing today? What is your regular schedule? Do you wake up at 11.00 AM? If you do, is it congruent with your vision? If it is not, write the bad habit on a separate piece of paper and circle it. This will mark the habit you need to change. Be thorough with this process.

* Pinpoint the activities you are currently not doing but are vital to your broad vision

Perhaps you intend to write a best seller before the lapse of five years. However, are you actually writing anything? (Small specs and recreational skits do not count here). If the answer is no, write the activity you must add to your day to make your goals a reality. After you do this, underline it.

* Break your 5-year vision into smaller one-year mini-visions that add up to the original five years. This gives you better control as well as an easier job of planning your action plan.

* For the 1-year mini visions, determine the time and effort you will require per day to make them a reality.

This should be easy; if it is not, break the year into individual months and weeks. Realistically, how much time per day can you spend working on your project? How much work must you complete to achieve your end year goal? Write this in a neat form. This should give you a very clear picture of what you want, and how to achieve it.

The First Step Is Always The Hardest

Steve Jobs hinted at this and so have so many other successful individuals. If anything, if you examine your life and some of the activities that have been most challenging to you, you may recognize this. You may realize that making that first move was the hard part. For instance, putting in that job application and then facing the interview panel may have been hard. From then on however, things became easier. This holds for goal setting and execution.

The first day will probably be the hardest to get through. You will thoroughly rationalize why you should not wake up at 5 am, why it is not worth it, and why it is possible to accomplish just as much by waking up two hours later. You will question your adherence to your own schedule. You will unfairly examine your timetable. You will question why you even have such high standards of living. You will ask yourself if you are ambitious or merely conceited to expect so much, even though you intend to work for it.

When your energy levels decrease after three hours of focus and work, you will try to convince yourself of the unworthiness of the pursuit. You will want to believe that life should be easy and effort free.

The first step or steps are usually the hardest. Yet if you remain persistent, everything becomes easier. You will be glad you did something about your life.

Step 2: Set Up And Execute That All-Important Yet Difficult First Step

Set up your first day of goal execution so that you wake up even earlier than you have planned

On that first day, you will have many "cobwebs" to brush off because for starters, you have not established a rhythm- you are just starting out. Even though you understand what needs doing, you will truly only know how much effort you expend after a full day's work. Wake up earlier to compensate for those periods of time you may spend in inactivity and uncertainty.

Plan and organize for everything you shall need for the next day

Whatever you need for the next day: clothes, stationery, working tools, and even motivational DVDs, keep them ready for tomorrow.

Befriend Caffeine

Caffeine is a great ally that will give you the extra edge you need to push past hard tasks.

For the first few days, work in small bursts with lots of rest phases

The fastest way to get discouraged is to set 4-hour working spans only to discover you can only work for one hour at optimum level. Have many rest phases in between small working periods. The starting period is delicate; go easy on yourself.

Make your own "company"

Artist Steve Keene, who has painted over 300,000 pieces, confessed that he keeps a radio system with tapes of talking people in his studio. The content is not important- just that the voices allow him to feel less lonely. Loneliness is the greatest work ethic killer there is.

Start with the difficult stuff and work your way to the easier ones

Starting with hard tasks and ending with easy ones means you tackle the hard stuff when you are at your freshest, which makes the tasks appear less difficult.

Begin the day with physical activity

This gives you one edge: conquering yourself physically opens your mind to conquering yourself in other ways. "So what if writing ten pages is difficult? I performed 50 pushups at 5.00 am when the rest of the world was asleep! Ten pages should be easy enough."

If you do not meet your day's objectives in the designated hours, work OT (overtime)

The auteur Nic Pizzolatto is famous for writing entire Grade A series scripts by himself, an incredible feat that often requires a writing panel of up to 10 people to accomplish. He says that if he does not cover the standard amount he sets for himself by dusk, he sticks around until he gets it done. When you are starting out, this will be a good tactic to adopt.

Why Most People Cannot Achieve Their Goals

Why do most people fail to achieve their goals? The reason is a phenomenon called "analysis paralysis".

Analysis paralysis is when you analyze what you have to do so thoroughly, and review it so completely that you start to hate the very thought of working on it. Too much analyzing paralyzes you. When you overanalyze, you ask too many questions and demand too much perfectionism. This makes it impossible to take the critical first step.

Does this sound familiar? Since you are reading this self-improvement book, it is fair to assume it does.

Analysis paralysis will kill your dreams. Analysis to the point where it paralyzes action demands unrealistic perfection. It is absurd to expect godlike results, as well as input when after all, you are human, even though you may be extremely good at what you do.

If you experience analysis paralysis, until you deal with it, you will never truly achieve anything you set out to. Even then, whispers of it will still linger. Thus, when dealing with analysis paralysis, you have to be very deliberate.

Step 3: Avoid Analysis Paralysis & In So Doing, Avoid The Slacker's Doom

To avoid analysis paralysis:

Just do it

You just have to put in the work. Granted, if you are the sort that examines his/her work very sternly, you will likely trash all that work if it does not meet your self-imposed high standard. Nevertheless, put in the work first and worry about the mistakes later when you are already doing something.

Plan your schedule to allow for uninterrupted input first followed by uninterrupted editing

The late great Georges Simenon, the author of 500 novels, wrote entire books for 11 days straight. For 11 days, he did no editing whatsoever. He then took three days off and launched himself into an entire week working on edits alone. When you constantly jog back to your work looking for that editable mistake, you run the risk of killing your drive. Therefore, work first, then correct mistakes later.

Cut down your "vocabulary"

Back Simenon again, he once said that the reason his material was so good, even when working on multiple books a year alone, was because he pared down his vocabulary to only 2,000 words. He took out all the fluff from his work. The very fluff that so many writers and artists cling to has been responsible for millions of unfinished works.

While you may be not be a writer, whatever your goals demand, pare down any fluff that may hold you back. Do this even in the preparation stages. Do you expect to have 5 teaspoons of sugar in your coffee, a hot bath, a banana and god-knows-what before you get started, and will not start until you do? Why must so many props be important? If the fridge has no bananas, settle for the coffee and buy the groceries later AFTER you have put in the work. The same applies to the sugar.

Work with another person with similar interests

A partner is often a good idea. When you work with someone, the added accountability makes it easier to feel motivated to work towards your goals.

Maintaining Energy And Motivation

We have talked about how to leap over the getting started hurdle. Now envision this: you are picking up momentum, having succeeded in getting started and are feeling good about yourself. You have incorporated the intermittent action system with rest phases in between the working periods. All seems to be well here: this goal-setting thing is not so hard after all, is it?

Then, before you know it, it is 1 pm, then 2 pm. You start to feel slower and lesser focused; your energy levels are dropping. Your concentration starts to worsen and you realize working in short bursts at a time is not working too well for you. How do you deal with this?

For starters, this is natural; embrace it as such. The other thing to know is that if you settle for here and end your working day, you are no better than the average slacker. You are no better than that fellow who does the same. Seeing you are this far in the book, you should be better.

You need to work on replenishing your depleted energy levels. Human beings have all these limitations; and so does everything that has the essence of life. There is, however, a silver lining? Just as much as depletion is a fact, so is recharging. Both go hand in hand. Whatever you deplete within you, you can always recharge. The solution will be to work on refilling your energy reserves.

Step 4: Revitalize Your Energy

To revitalize your energy and motivation:

Keep caffeine handy

We have previously talked about coffee in this book; here it is again. Coffee does well to revitalize you and to increase your energy levels. On the downside, the effects of caffeine wear off after a couple of hours and you will need another shot. Still, a few hours are more than enough time to complete immense amounts of work.

Additionally, if you can interrupt the pattern of laziness the body has adopted (usually at or after lunchtime), you may find that the urge to slack off has worn off after the coffee stimulation wears off.

Coffee contains the stimulant caffeine, a mildly addictive stimulant. Caffeine stimulates your system and enhances blood flow to critical parts of your body (such as the brain). The stimulating effect causes your brain to be more alert; the result is feeling more pumped up.

Load up on fish oil

Fish oil is very effective and is great for building your brain. When your body breaks it down, it converts it into energy that will allow you to work. Oils and fats are some of the best energy giving foods. Actually, oils will give you about as three times the amount of energy per gram as carbohydrates.

Further, to synthesize fat, your body does not need to work overtime.

The trick is to find the right kind of fats and oils, fats and oils that will not contribute to obesity and cholesterol problems. Fish oil is at the top of this pile.

Drink lots of water throughout

Do you know why you often feel sluggish? It is because you are dehydrated. When your body is dehydrated, it starts acting like a miser with the water reserves it has available. It holds onto more water than it should and the accumulated effect is that you feel especially slow. You will also look bloated and puffy.

Include A healthy serving of greens in your lunch

Even if you eat lots of them, veggies are not as high in calories as carbohydrates. Yet, when the body breaks them down, they will give you sufficient energy. What is more, they will have a great impact on your immune system. It is no secret that you will do more when you are healthy.

Tapping Into The Conscious Mind

They say everything you take in, be it via the eyes or the ears never leaves your mind. Every tiny memory and piece of information lodges itself in your mind, never to leave. Every action you witness, every plan you make, and everything that makes an impression on your mind leaves an imprint on your brain.

If the brain is like a fishnet where every impression comes in yet cannot leave, why is it that you have trouble remembering many things? It is because the bulk of your memory storage is in the subconscious mind. Your mind, being the efficient tool it is, only keeps that which it deems as most important in your conscious memory, available for easy retrieval and examination.

All you have to do is impress upon your conscious mind that your goals are too important to be lumped in the subconscious memory. Once you have succeeded in doing this, it will become easy to recall thoughts related to your goals. You will find it easy to examine their congruency with the present time, and understand what you need to change.

Step 5: Enhance Conscious Awareness Of Your Goals

To keep the conscious mind from putting your important goals with other memories going into storage into the subconscious mind, you have to

Get into the habit of reading your goals aloud daily

When you do this, you commit your goals to the working memory. Reading your goals aloud makes it easier to remember them because you have so much more attached: you will remember the tone of your voice and this help you to remember the words you read aloud.

Put in good old fashioned work

Actions speak louder than words. When you set about working on your goals on a daily basis, the habit will become so ingrained that thinking about your goals, and their importance, will be second nature. When you take a day off, your brain will be sending signals that there is something missing from your day. Even in the breaks between your working periods, you will find your mind drifting towards your goals, and your goal achievement process. This will be a very potent spur.

Act as if you have already accomplished your goals so a pattern establishes in your mind

Take the example of body builders. When they "shock" the muscle by lifting a weight that is heavier, the body adapts and behaves as if that particular weight is the normal weight. In so doing, it tears whatever muscle tissue exists and builds newer, stronger, and bigger muscle tissue. It adapts to survive. The circle extends to the rest of the body, mind included.

Your body will adapt to survive in whatever environment you thrust it into, be it a physical or mental environment. Once you behave as if you are successful, the body adapts itself very quickly to suit your mindset. You start questioning yourself for waking up late, not following up on your goals, slacking off, and whatever else that contravenes the success you aim to achieve. This counter effect pushes your goals to the forefront of your mind.

Be consistent and work towards your goals every day

Establish a habit. Your mind is not stupid- it will easily identify the link between your action and the goals you are striving to achieve.

Leaping Over Inevitable Blocks

It is hard to understand why 'they' only found a name for the block writers experience (writer's block) and skipped just about every other occupation, even though blocks are just as common there. You should expect to have spells of time where you will feel your creative capacity being at its lowest point.

When this happens, contrary to what so many motivational books will have you believe, the solution is not to pack and wait for the next wave of inspiration. This will just make you a slave of your own limitations (take the phrase limitation with a grain of salt here). You must aggressively face the creative block you face. Unbelievably, this hurdle is a lot easier to navigate than you may think.

Step 6: Overcome Creative Blocks

To overcome creative blocks:

Shock your body with an impromptu exercise

Drop down and push off 10 rapid pushups before heading back to your desk. What you accomplish here is that you jerk your system from the lull it had settled in. Suddenly, more blood is flowing through your veins and into your head. This makes it easier to think creatively.

Hydrate

Every time you drink water, you may note that you feel a lot fresher and eager to get going. Hydrating your body has a way of purifying your system, allowing your body to function at optimum level.

Wash your face and head

Always keep a small face towel in your bag. Every time the creative block is especially stubborn, take it out, run some water on the towel and wipe your face and head. You will be amazed at how much fresher you feel.

Focus on another thread

This means you should focus on another task, preferably one that is relevant to the one at hand. When you move your brain into a different creative direction, you stimulate it away from the block. Once you get back to your task, it will be easier to process new ideas.

Get working

Move away from the need to produce something perfect and just move forward with whatever flimsy ideas you may have available. Granted, you may have to delete a vast amount of what you do, but at least, you will have a base you can build upon. This step also gives you total power over creative blocks, to a point where they stop intimidating you ever again.

Accomplishing Your Goals: 3-Week Action Plan

Before we move on, you should know that the action plan becomes progressively more demanding with each 3-day set. By day 19 to day 21 set, it will be quite demanding, with working days ending at 7.00 pm.

If you cannot keep up with the rigors of the last set after day 21, do not be too hard on yourself. However, you must accomplish this routine play for play until the 21 days lapse. After that, you will know what works for you and how you should design your working days.

Day 1 to Day 3

* Wake up at 5.30 am.

* Jog for 5 minutes before heading back indoors.

* Follow this routine with 5 pushups.

* Drink a mug of coffee and follow up with sufficient hydration (drink two glasses of water). You should organize this to coincide with your breakfast time.

* At 8.25 am, clear your workstation so by 8.30, you are set to begin working.

* Settle down for work and for thirty minutes, work uninterrupted.

How To Set Goals For Yourself

* After thirty minutes of focused work, take a 15-minute break.

* Get back to your workstation promptly and work for an extra 30 minutes.

* Take yet another 15-minute break from your workstation.

* Repeat your 30-minute work session. As you work, limit interruptions around you.

* As you work, ensure your email and message notifications are off and direct all calls to voicemail for the 30-minute period. Switch them on for the 15-minute breaks, tend to them, and then switch them off when the 30-minute work cycle commences again.

* At lunchtime, take the hour off.

* During the last 5 minutes of the free hour, perform a set of light stretching exercises.

* Get back to the 30-minute work periods with 15-minute breaks.

* Wrap up your workday up at 4.00 pm.

Day 4 to Day 6

* Wake up at 5.15 am.

* Jog for 10 minutes before heading back indoors.

* Follow this routine with 10 pushups.

* Drink a mug of coffee and follow it up with sufficient hydration (drink three glasses of water). You should organize this to coincide with your breakfast time.

* At 8.15 am, clear your workstation so that by 8.20, you are ready to begin working.

* Settle down for work and for forty-five minutes, work uninterrupted.

* After your 45 minutes focused work session, take a 10-minute break.

* Get back to your workstation promptly and work for an extra 45 minutes.

* Take yet another 10-minute break from your workstation.

* Repeat your 45-minute work session. As you work, ensure minimal interruptions.

* Turn of your email and text notification and direct all calls to voicemail for the 45-minute focused work period. Switch on these services during the 10-minute breaks, tend to them,

and then switch them off when the 45-minute work cycle commences.

* At lunch, take 45-minutes off.

* During the last 10 minutes of the free 45 minutes, perform a set of light stretching exercises to stimulate you.

* Get back to the 45-minute work periods with 10-minute breaks.

* Wrap up your workday at 4.30 pm.

Day 7 to Day 9

* Wake up at 5.00 am.

* Jog for 15 minutes before heading indoors.

* Follow this routine with 15 pushups.

* Drink a mug of coffee and follow this up with sufficient hydration (drink two glasses of water). You should organize this to coincide with your breakfast time.

* At 8.05 am, clear your workstation and by 8.10, to begin working.

* Settle down for work and for one hour, work uninterrupted.

* After one hour of uninterrupted work, take a 10-minute break.

* Get back to your workstation promptly after the 10-minutes break and work for another one hour.

* Take yet another 10-minute break from your workstation.

* Repeat your one-hour work session. As you work, eliminate all distraction..

* At lunch hour, take 45-minutes off.

* During the last 10 minutes of the 45-minute break, perform a set of light stretching exercises and to stimulate your body. Get back to the one hour work periods with 10 minute breaks.

* Wrap up your workday at 5.00 pm.

Day 10 to Day 12

* Wake up at 5.00 am.

* Jog for 20 minutes before heading back indoors.

* Follow this routine with 15 pushups.

* Drink a mug of coffee followed by sufficient hydration (drink four glasses of water). You should organize this to coincide with your breakfast time.

* At 7.55 am, clear your workstation; by 8.00, be ready to start working.

How To Set Goals For Yourself

* Settle down for work and for one hour and thirty minutes, work uninterrupted.

* After working for one hour and thirty minutes, take a 10-minute break.

* When the break lapses, promptly get back to your workstation and work for a one-hour period.

* Take yet another 10-minute break from your workstation.

* Head back to your workstation and work for one hour and thirty minutes. As you work, limit all interruptions. The idea is to keep the cycle going- you work for one and a half hour, a ten-minute break, followed by one-hour work period followed by 10-minute break then 1 ½-hour work period.

* As you work, ensure all email alerts are off, text notification, and direct all calls to voicemail. Switch on these services for first 10-minute break, tend to them, and then switch them off when the one-hour of work starts. However, after the one hour of work, do not switch on the email service, texts, and calls. Only switch them on after the alternating one and a half hour period.

* At lunchtime, take 40-minutes off.

* During the last 10 minutes of the 40-minute break, perform a set of light stretching exercises to stimulate your body. Get back to the 1 ½ hour- one hour alternating work periods with 10 minute breaks.

* Wrap up your workday up at 5.00 pm.

How To Set Goals For Yourself

Day 13 to Day 15

* Wake up at 5.00 am

* Jog for 25 minutes before heading indoors

* Follow this routine with 15 pushups.

* Drink a mug of coffee and follow this with drinking four glasses of water.

* At 7.25 am, clear your workstation. By 7.30 am, begin working.

* Settle down for work and for two hours, work uninterrupted.

* After your two hours of work, take a 10-minute break.

* Get back to your workstation promptly after the 10-minute break and work for a one-hour period.

* Take yet another 10-minute break from your workstation.

* Head back to your workstation and work for two hours. As you work, minimize all distractions.

* Keep the cycle going: work for a two-hour period followed a 10-minute break, followed by a one-hour of work, a 10-minute break, and so forth.

* At lunchtime, take 40-minutes off.

* During the last 10 minutes of the 40 minutes, perform a set of light stretching exercises. Get back to the two hour- one hour alternating work periods with 10-minute breaks.

* Wrap up your workday at 5.00 pm.

Day 16 to Day 18

* Wake up at 5.00 am

* Jog for 25 minutes before heading indoors

* Follow this routine with 15 pushups.

* Drink a mug of coffee and four glasses of water.

* At 7.05 am, clear your workstation, and by 7.10 am, start working.

* For two hours, work uninterrupted.

* After the two hours of work, take a 20-minute break.

* Get back to your workstation promptly after the 20-minutes break and work for another 2-hour period.

* Take yet another 20-minute break from your workstation.

* Head back to your workstation and work for two hours. As you work, minimize all distractions. The idea is to keep the cycle going: work for a two-hour period, take a 20-minute break, follow this with a two-hour work period, take 20 minutes break, follow up with another two-hour period, and so forth.

* At lunchtime, take 45 minutes off.

* During the last 10 minutes of the 45-minutes break, perform a set of light stretching exercises. Get back to the two-hour work periods with 20-minute breaks, making sure to switch off your email service, phone calls, and text messaging accordingly.

* Wrap up your workday up at 5.00 pm.

Day 19 to Day 21

* Wake up at 5.00 am

* Jog for 30 minutes before heading indoors. Follow this with 15 pushups.

* Drink a mug of coffee and five glasses of water. Tweak this to coincide with your breakfast time.

* At 7.00 am, clear your workstation so that by 7.05 am, you are ready to begin working.

* Settle down for work and for two hours, work uninterrupted.

* After working for two hours, take a 15-minute break.

* Get back to your workstation after the 15-minute break and work for another 2-hour period.

How To Set Goals For Yourself

* Take yet another 15-minute break from your workstation.

* Immediately after the break, head back to your workstation and work for two hours. As you work, ensure minimal interruptions.

* At lunchtime, take 45 minutes off. During the last 10 minutes of the 45 minutes, perform a set of light stretching exercises. Get back to the two-hour work periods with 20-minute breaks.

* Wrap up your workday up at 5.00 pm.

Conclusion

Thank you again for downloading this book!

As clearly shown in this book, it is not hard to set relevant goals and follow through to achieve a higher quality of life. The only thing you need to do is understand how to go about creating goals and accomplishing them. In that respect, this book has given you everything you need to live a goal driven life.

Finally, if you enjoyed this book, would you be kind enough to leave a review for this book on Amazon?

Please post a review of this book on Amazon.

Thank you and good luck!

Do You Like My Book & Approach To Publishing?

If you like my writing and style and would love the ease of learning literally everything you can get your hands on from Fantonpublishers.com, I'd really need you to do me either of the following favors.

1: First, I'd Love It If You Leave a Review of This Book on Amazon.

2: Grab Some Freebies On Your Way Out; Giving Is Receiving, Right?

I gave you a complimentary book at the start of the book. If you are still interested, grab it here.

[5 Pillar Life Transformation Checklist](http://bit.ly/2fantonfreebie): http://bit.ly/2fantonfreebie

3: Check Out My Other Books On Productivity

How To Set Goals For Yourself

Habit Building: How To Build Good Habits to Transform Your Life and Create Lasting Change without Feeling Overwhelmed and Frustrated

Procrastination Cure: Stop Being Lazy, Get Stuff Done, Master Your Time, Increase Your Productivity And Level Up by Beating Procrastination

www.ingramcontent.com/pod-product-compliance
Lightning Source LLC
Chambersburg PA
CBHW050841040426
42333CB00058B/393